Culture & Leisure Services
Red Doles Lane
Huddersfield, West Yorks. HD2 1YF

THE **FESTIVE** FOOD OF

China

BY DEH-TA HSIUNG

Photography by
Will Heap

Kyle Cathie Limited

This edition first published in Great Britain 2006 by
Kyle Cathie Limited
122 Arlington Road
London NW1 7HP
www.kylecathie.com

ISBN 1 85626 683 4
ISBN (13-digit) 978 1 85626 683 3

Originally published 1991

Designed by **pinkstripedesign.com**

Photography by **Will Heap**

Illustrations by **Sally Maltby**

Home economy by **Annie Nichols and Jacque Malouf**

Styling by **Roisin Nield**

Production by **Sha Huxtable & Alice Holloway**

A Cataloguing in Publication record for this title is available from the
British Library.

Reproduction by Image Scanhouse
Printed and bound in China by SNP Leefung Printers Limited

**Recipes are for 4–6 people when served on their
own or 10–12 when combined with two or three
other dishes.**

Previous page and this page: Istock Images

CONTENTS

LITTLE NEW YEAR

The festivities for New Year in parts of China start during the last week of the old year – a period known as Little New Year. On the twenty-third or twenty-fourth of the twelfth moon, families gather in front of the Kitchen God, the household's guardian angel. During the rest of the year his statue, picture or tablet lives on the chimney breast, but on this night he is carried into the courtyard by the head of the family and set on fire. This practice sends him to heaven to report on the deeds of his family. Accompanied by the noise of loud firecrackers and with his lips smeared with honey, molasses or sticky sweets to ensure he can only report sweet things or, perhaps, to seal them so that he cannot say anything at all, he is given a great send-off.

Once he has departed, a small feast is served, and feasts and festivities continue for the next seven days, until the grand feast on New Year's Eve. One special dish served during Little New Year is the Chinese version of a fondue.

left New Year firecrackers, Randy Faris/Corbis

CHINESE HOT POT

This is a complete meal in itself. You can find an authentic charcoal or spirit-burning hot pot at most Oriental stores.

225g chicken breast meat
  (boned and skinned)
450g lamb fillet
  (or pork, beef or all), trimmed
55g Chinese dried mushrooms,
  soaked in warm water for
  30–40 minutes
450g Chinese leaves or spinach
200g–300g bean curd (tofu)
255g bean thread noodles
225g peeled prawns
2 litres chicken or meat stock
  or water

DIPPING SAUCE
100ml light soy sauce
75ml dark soy sauce
55g sugar
3–4 spring onions,
  finely chopped
3–4 slices fresh ginger root,
  peeled and finely chopped
2 garlic cloves, crushed and
  finely chopped (optional)
2 teaspoons sesame oil
chilli sauce (optional)

serves 6–8

1 Trim the chicken and lamb and cut into wafer-thin slices.

2 Squeeze the mushrooms dry and discard the stalks. Cut the mushrooms, Chinese leaves and bean curd into small pieces.

3 Soak the noodles for 5–10 minutes until soft.

4 Arrange all the prepared ingredients either on a large plate or on small individual dishes. Arrange the ingredients for the dipping sauce on the table ready for the diners to mix them, according to their taste.

5 When you are ready to eat, bring the stock or water to a boil in the hot pot at the table. Each person should then pick up a piece of meat with chopsticks and dip it into the boiling liquid for no more than a few seconds, until the colour of the meat changes – and then quickly dip it in the sauce.

6 When the meats have been eaten, add the vegetables to the pot. Boil for a few minutes, season the liquid with the remaining dip sauce, and serve the soup to finish the meal.

NEW YEAR'S EVE GRAND FEAST

New Year's Eve is probably the festival of the year: a time for settling debts in order to start the New Year with a clean slate, and, equally important, a time when all the family gathers together to relax and to enjoy themselves. The Kitchen God is ceremoniously welcomed back with red candles, incense, firecrackers and offerings of pork, chicken or duck, carp, wine and fruits. The new effigy is placed in its shrine on the chimney breast and then the whole family sits down to a huge feast.

The feast starts with a couple of deep-fried dishes followed by a soup and duck, which is considered special, a leg or hand of pork and, to complete the traditional 'three meats', carp is always included for New Year as it is the fish of good fortune. A bowl or two of vegetables are always served at any Chinese meal with rice, to fill the empty corners.

left Incense sticks burning, Gavin Hellier/Robert Harding World Images/Getty Images **right** Firecrackers, Grant Faint/The Image Bank/Getty Images

BUTTERFLY PRAWNS

For best results, use uncooked king prawns in their shells. Sold headless, they are 8–10cm long, and you should get 18–20 prawns per 450g.

450g headless king prawns
   in their shells
1 tablespoon light soy sauce
1 teaspoon ground Sichuan
   pepper
3 tablespoons Shao Hsing rice
   wine or dry sherry
2 teaspoons cornflour
2 eggs, lightly beaten
30g breadcrumbs
about 575ml oil for deep-frying
lettuce leaves
2–3 spring onions, shredded,
   to garnish

1 Shell the prawns but leave the tails on. Split them in half from the underbelly about three-quarters of the way through, leaving the tails still firmly attached. Marinate in the soy sauce, pepper, wine and cornflour for 10–15 minutes.

2 Pick up a prawn by the tail, dip it in the egg then roll it in the breadcrumbs before lowering it into medium-hot oil. Deep-fry the prawns in batches until golden brown. Remove and drain.

3 To serve, arrange the prawns neatly on a bed of lettuce leaves and garnish with spring onions.

CHICKEN WITH LEMON SAUCE

550g chicken breast meat
1 or 2 eggs, lightly beaten
3½ tablespoons cornflour
about 575ml oil for deep-frying
200ml bottled lemon sauce from
  Oriental stores
slices of fresh lemon to garnish

1 Trim the chicken breasts, coat with egg and cornflour and deep-fry in hot oil, until golden. Remove and drain.

2 Cut each breast into bite-sized pieces and arrange on a hot serving plate.

3 Heat about 1 tablespoon oil in a saucepan and mix in the lemon sauce, blend well and pour evenly over the chicken. Garnish with lemon slices and serve hot.

EIGHT-TREASURE SOUP

30g Chinese dried mushrooms,
   soaked for 35–40 minutes in
   warm water
30g dried shrimps, soaked for
   25–30 minutes in warm water
700ml chicken or meat stock
55g chicken meat, thinly
   shredded
55g pork fillet, thinly shredded
55g bamboo shoots, thinly
   shredded
55g spinach leaves, thinly
   shredded
100g bean curd (tofu), sliced
1½ tablespoons light soy sauce
2 eggs, lightly beaten
1 tablespoon cornflour mixed
   with an equal amount of water
salt and pepper
finely chopped spring onion to
   garnish

1 Squeeze the mushrooms dry, discard the stalks and shred finely. Rinse and drain the shrimps.

2 Bring the stock to a rolling boil, add the shrimps, chicken, pork and mushrooms, stir to separate, then add bamboo shoots, spinach, bean curd and soy sauce. Bring back to the boil and pour in the eggs.

3 Thicken the soup with the cornflour and water mixture. Cook for a further 1 minute. Adjust the seasoning, garnish with spring onions and serve hot.

ROAST DUCK WITH STUFFING

1 duckling, weighing 2kg,
   cleaned
3 tablespoons dark soy sauce

STUFFING
115g glutinous rice or
   round pudding rice
4–5 medium Chinese dried
   mushrooms
30g dried shrimps
giblets (gizzard, heart and liver)
   of the duck
55g bamboo shoots
55g cooked ham
1½ tablespoons oil
2 spring onions, finely chopped
1 tablespoon light soy sauce
1 tablespoon Shao Hsing rice
   wine or dry sherry
salt to taste

1 Brush the duck skin with the dark soy sauce.

2 Soak the rice in 175ml boiling water for 20–25 minutes. Soak the dried mushrooms in warm water for 25–30 minutes, squeeze dry and, discarding the stalks, cut into pea-sized cubes. Soak the dried shrimps in warm water for 20 minutes, rinse and drain. Boil the gizzard gently in water for 10–15 minutes and dice, along with the heart, liver, bamboo shoots and ham.

3 Heat the oil in a wok and stir-fry the mushrooms, shrimps, giblets, bamboo shoots, ham and spring onions for 1 minute. Mix in the light soy sauce and wine, the rice and its soaking water and salt. Bring to the boil, then reduce heat and cook for 8–10 minutes, or until all the liquid is absorbed.

4 Preheat the oven to 200°C/400°F/gas 6. Pack the stuffing into the duck cavity and close up the tail opening. Place the duck on a wire rack in a roasting tin and cook in the oven for 30 minutes, then reduce the heat to 180°C/350°F/gas 4 and cook for a further 45 minutes.

5 To serve, scrape out the stuffing and spread out on a platter, chop the duck into bite-sized pieces and arrange neatly on top of the stuffing.

RED-COOKED LEG OR SHOULDER OF PORK

South of the Yangtze River, where pork is plentiful, this dish is a must for every feast and is the nearest equivalent to the British Sunday joint. Leg of mutton or shin of beef, cut into large chunks, can also be cooked this way.

1.35–1.5kg leg or
  shoulder of pork,
  cleaned
4–5 spring onions
3–4 slices of fresh
  ginger root
3 tablespoons light
  soy sauce
100ml dark soy sauce
3 tablespoons brandy
115g rock candy or
  crystal sugar

1 Make sure the pork skin is free of bristles and then score the rind and meat with a few cuts.

2 Place the meat with the spring onions and ginger in a large saucepan, skin-side down. Cover with cold water and bring to the boil rapidly, skimming constantly. Add the soy sauces and brandy, reduce the heat and simmer, covered, for 30 minutes.

3 Turn the meat over, add the sugar, cover and continue cooking for about 1½ hours. Now reduce the liquor by boiling rapidly, uncovered, for 5–10 minutes.

4 To serve, lift out the meat and place on a deep serving dish, skin-side up. Discard the ginger and spring onions and pour the gravy over the pork. The meat should be tender enough to tear into shreds with chopsticks.

right Alain Evrard/Lonely Planet Images/Getty Images

STEAMED WHOLE FISH

The last main course of any feast must include a whole fish because the Chinese word for fish, *yu*, is pronounced the same as the word 'to spare' – and we like to think that there is always something on the table to spare, particularly on New Year's Eve for the start of the New Year.

1 scaled and gutted carp,
   sea bass, trout or grey mullet,
   weighing about 700g (or 2
   smaller ones)
1 teaspoon salt
2 teaspoons sesame oil
2–3 spring onions, cut in half
   lengthways
2 slices fresh ginger root, peeled
   and finely shredded
1½ tablespoons light soy sauce
1½ tablespoons Shao Hsing rice
   wine or dry sherry
1 tablespoon oil
finely shredded spring onions
   to garnish

1 Clean the fish well and dry thoroughly. Score both sides of the fish as far as the bone with diagonal cuts at 1cm intervals. Rub the inside and outside of the fish with salt and sesame oil. Place it on top of the spring onions on a heatproof platter and then place the ginger on top of the fish.

2 Put the platter in a hot steamer or inside a wok on a rack, and steam vigorously for 15–18 minutes.

3 Remove the platter from the steamer and pour the soy sauce and wine evenly over the fish; meanwhile, heat the oil until hot. Place the finely shredded spring onions on top of the fish, then pour the hot oil over the whole length of the fish. Serve immediately.

BRAISED CHINESE VEGETABLES

30g wood ears (dried black
  fungus)
115g bamboo shoots or carrots
115g broccoli or mange tout
225g Chinese leaves
115g beansprouts or
  celery hearts
1 small red pepper, cored
  and deseeded
3 tablespoons oil
1 teaspoon salt
1 teaspoon sugar
1 tablespoon light soy sauce
sesame oil to garnish

1 Soak the dried fungus in warm water for 10–15 minutes, rinse and drain. Roughly dice the fresh vegetables.

2 Heat the oil in a wok, add the carrots first, if using, followed by broccoli or mange tout and Chinese leaves about 1 minute later. Add the rest of the vegetables and stir-fry for about 2 minutes. Now add salt and sugar, and a little stock or water if necessary. Continue stirring for a further 1 minute or so, then add the soy sauce and sesame oil. Serve hot or cold.

NEW YEAR'S DAY

The traditional Chinese calendar is based on the cycles of the moon. The words 'month' and 'moon' are identical because, according to our Chinese lunar calendar, one month equals one moon. The number of days in a month corresponds to the number of days it takes the moon to make one complete revolution around the earth. So some months have twenty-nine days, others thirty days; but the new moon is always on the first of the month and the full moon on the fifteenth day.

New Year's Day is celebrated by children everywhere as their birthday. I remember the excitement, the presents, toys and clothes, the little red envelopes I found tucked under my pillow bulging with money.

This is also the day when the gods are honoured with lighted red candles and incense, when food and inscriptions written on red paper are placed in their shrines and everyone wears new clothes. The day starts with a bang of firecrackers to mark the 'Opening the Door to Welcome the Auspicious New Year' ceremony.

Afterwards, throughout the day, people call on each other offering the compliments of the season. They are given tea and the Eight-treasure Box – an octagonal box divided into eight sections containing sweetmeats and nuts. Close relatives and special guests are also offered New Year Cakes or, in the north, Jiao Zi – wheat flour dumplings.

NEW YEAR CAKE

This basic New Year Cake recipe is served with sugar or syrup, but other sweet fillings, all offering different colours and fragrances, include sesame seed paste, red or black bean paste, or honey.

450g glutinous rice flour
225g brown sugar
about 350ml boiling water
30g lard
oil for frying

1 Sift the flour into a bowl. Dissolve the sugar in the water and slowly add to the flour, mixing to a smooth consistency.

2 Grease a 20cm cake tin with the lard and fill with the dough. Steam over rapidly boiling water for about 2 hours. Remove and invert onto a plate. When cool, refrigerate, well covered, for at least 6–8 hours to harden.

3 To serve, cut the cake into diamond-shaped pieces and shallow-fry in oil on both sides until brown. Serve hot with either caster sugar or golden syrup.

left Chinese Buddhist Shrine, Bohemian Nomad Picturemakers/Corbis

JIAO ZI

PEKING DUMPLINGS

Jiao Zi are eaten for breakfast on New Year's Day. Most households make enough to last four or five days, and leave the uncooked Jiao Zi outside to freeze in the bitterly cold winter, using them from frozen as required.

DOUGH
450g plain flour
about 450ml water
flour for dusting

FILLING
450g Chinese leaves or
  white cabbage
450g pork or lamb, minced
3 spring onions, finely chopped
1 teaspoon finely chopped
  fresh ginger root
2 teaspoons salt
1 teaspoon sugar
1½ tablespoons light soy sauce
1 tablespoon Shao Hsing
  rice wine
2 teaspoons sesame oil

DIPPING SAUCE
2–3 slices fresh ginger root,
  finely shredded
60ml rice vinegar
1½ tablespoons light soy sauce

1 Sift the flour into a bowl, slowly pour in the water and mix to a firm dough. Knead until smooth and soft. Cover with a damp cloth and set aside for 25–30 minutes.

2 Blanch the cabbage leaves until soft; drain and chop finely. Mix in the remaining filling ingredients and blend well.

3 Lightly dust a work surface with flour, knead and roll the dough into a long sausage of about 2.5cm diameter. Cut into 80–90 small pieces. Flatten each piece with the palm of your hand, then with a rolling pin roll out each into a pancake about 6cm in diameter.

4 Place about 1 tablespoon of filling in the centre of each pancake and fold it into a half-moon-shaped pouch, then pinch the edges firmly so that the dumpling is tightly sealed.

5 Make the dipping sauce by mixing all the ingredients together.

6 Bring about 2 litres water to a rolling boil and drop in about 20 dumplings, stirring gently with chopsticks to prevent them sticking together. Cover, bring back to the boil and then add about 150ml cold water; bring to the boil again, this time uncovered. Repeat twice more, remove the dumplings with a strainer and serve hot with the dipping sauce. Store any uncooked Jiao Zi in the freezer.

LANTERN FESTIVAL

The Lantern Festival or Big New Year, on the fifteenth day of the first moon, dates from the rule of the Emperor Ming (58–75 AD) of the Han Dynasty, and formally ends the New Year celebrations, marking the return of the spring light and the lengthening of the day.

Lanterns are lit all over the country in homes and temples and spectacular processions of exquisite silk and paper lanterns in every shape and form take place in the streets; at the end of each procession a magnificent dragon, carried by at least a dozen men, dances to the deafening rhythm of cymbals and drums and firecrackers.

Traditionally, Tang Yuan, little round dumplings made of glutinous rice powder, are eaten.

left Chinese lanterns, Jake Wyman/Photonica/Getty Images

Tang Yuan

These little round dumplings owe their origin to the famous snacks known as wontons in the West.

DOUGH
50g sago, soaked for 6 hours in cold water
225g glutinous rice flour
about 300ml cold water

FILLING
225g pork, coarsely minced
pinch of salt
1 teaspoon sugar
1 tablespoon light soy sauce
1 tablespoon Shao Hsing rice wine
1 spring onion, finely chopped

makes 16 dumplings

1 Drain the sago in a sieve for 30 minutes and mix with the glutinous rice flour. Add the cold water and knead until the dough is smooth.

2 Mix together all the ingredients for the filling. Set aside for 30–35 minutes.

3 Roll the dough into a long sausage shape, about 2.5cm in diameter, and cut into 1cm pieces. Flatten each piece of dough and place about ½ teaspoon filling in the centre. Carefully draw the edges of dough over the filling, seal and shape into a small ball by rolling between the palms of your hands. The dumplings may be made in advance and refrigerated.

4 For four servings: bring about 700ml water to a rolling boil, drop in 16 dumplings, one by one, and stir very gently to prevent them from sticking together. Cook vigorously until they all float to the surface, then reduce the heat and simmer for 5 minutes. Scoop them into individual bowls and cover with some of the water. Serve hot.

BIRTHDAY OF GUAN YIN

The birthday of the Goddess of Mercy, Guan Yin, is celebrated on the nineteenth day of the second moon.

There are many stories about her origins. In one legend she was the daughter of an Indian prince and a disciple of Gautama, the Buddha. In another she was born in the third century BC as the Chinese daughter of one of the Zhou Emperors and became a nun.

The name 'Guan Yin' also means 'observing or taking note of sounds' and, as such, she is worshipped by both Buddhists and Taoists, appealing primarily to women. They pray to her for prosperity, security and male children. Some devout women even observe a period of fasting – giving up meat, fish, poultry, eggs and dairy products – from the beginning of the second moon until her birthday.

On the dawn of the nineteenth, Guan Yin's shrines are crowded with her followers bringing gifts and food and, although you may find chicken, duck or fish, for the truly devout, vegetarian food is the order of the day.

GUAN YIN TANG MEIN

VEGETARIAN NOODLES IN SOUP

This dish owes its origin to Buddhist temples and monasteries where it would be offered by the monks and nuns to visiting worshippers.

30g dried bean curd
   (tofu) skin
3–4 Chinese dried mushrooms
30g dried tiger lily buds
   (Golden Needles)
225g fine rice noodles
   (vermicelli)
50ml oil
55g water chestnuts, cut into
   thin strips
55g bamboo shoots, cut into
   thin strips
55g carrots, cut into thin strips
55g spinach or lettuce
   leaves, cut into thin strips
½ teaspoon salt
1 teaspoon sugar
1½ tablespoons light soy sauce
1 teaspoon sesame oil
thinly shredded spring onions
   to garnish

1 Soak the bean curd skin in cold water for 4–6 hours, or in warm water for 2–3 hours, then slice thinly. Soak the mushrooms in warm water for 30–40 minutes, squeeze dry (reserve the water), discard the stalks and cut into thin slices. Soak the lily buds in cold water for 20–30 minutes and rinse until clear.

2 Cook the noodles in boiling water following the instructions on the packet; drain (reserve the water) and place them in a large serving bowl. Pour enough of the cooking liquid into the bowl to half-cover the noodles. Keep warm.

3 Heat the oil in a wok, stir-fry the vegetables for about 2 minutes, add the salt, sugar, soy sauce and a little of the mushroom-soaking water. Bring to the boil, add the sesame oil and then pour all the vegetables and liquid over the noodles. Garnish with spring onions and serve hot.

BIRTHDAY OF THE GODDESS OF THE SEA

The birthday of Mazu, the Holy Mother and Goddess of the Sea, is celebrated on the twenty-third day of the third moon. The daughter of a fisherman from Fujian, she is also known as Tian Hou (The Queen of Heaven).

One day when her parents were out fishing, she fell into a trance and saw that they were in grave danger; a storm was raging and their boat was tossing and turning at sea. Rushing down to the beach, she could just see them on the horizon. Fixing her eyes on their tiny boat, she guided them safely back to the shore whilst boats all around them were sinking.

From that day, the fishing communities stretching from Fujian in the south east to Taiwan and Hong Kong have prayed to her for protection, for fair weather and a good catch; and there are shrines and temples dedicated to her on every junk and village sea front. On Mazu's birthday the fishermen make pilgrimages to temples dedicated to her in the ports of Fuzhou, Xiamen and Zhaoan.

The daily diet of the fishing folk consists mainly of fish and vegetables, so a festival day offers a rare excuse to eat meat.

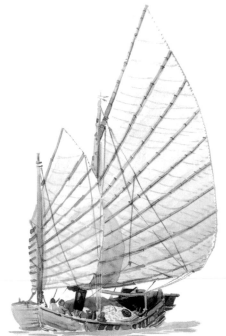

LONG-BRAISED PORK
WITH BAMBOO SHOOTS

For this popular way of cooking pork and bamboo shoots in south China, the pork should not be too lean, so the bamboo shoots can soak up the excess fat. It can be cooked well in advance and be reheated just before serving.

1kg belly pork
450g bamboo shoots
1½ tablespoons oil
3 tablespoons light soy sauce
1½ tablespoons dark soy sauce
3 tablespoons Shao Hsing
   rice wine
1 tablespoon sugar
1 teaspoon five-spice powder

1 Cut the pork into 2.5cm cubes. Cut the bamboo shoots into triangular-shaped chunks of the same size.

2 Blanch the pork by immersing in a pan of boiling water and removing as soon as the water starts to boil again. Rinse the pork in cold water and drain.

3 Heat the oil in a large saucepan or pot and stir-fry the pork for about 30 seconds, then add the soy sauces, wine, sugar and just enough water to cover. Bring to the boil, reduce the heat and simmer gently, covered, for 1 hour, turning once or twice.

4 Add the bamboo shoots and five-spice powder, blending well. Cook for a further 30 minutes or so under cover. Serve hot.

QING MING

left A man prays during the Quing Ming festival, Sam Yeh/AFP/Getty Images

Qing Ming means 'pure and clean' and is the name given to the time when families visit and spring clean their relatives' graves in the countryside and bring food and other offerings for the departed.

As Qing Ming falls exactly 106 days after the winter solstice, the weather is mild, and after the graves have been tidied and the proper respects paid, most families spoil themselves with a picnic. Only cold food, prepared in advance, is eaten; out of respect for the dead, no fires are lit in the homes for at least two days.

'WHITE-CUT' CHICKEN

There are many variations of this famous Cantonese recipe.
But whichever version you try, always use a fresh young chicken.

1 young chicken,
   weighing 1.35kg
2 spring onions, each tied
   into a knot
2 slices fresh ginger root, crushed
1 teaspoon Sichuan peppercorns
2 teaspoons salt

SAUCE
3 tablespoons light soy sauce
1½ tablespoons Shao Hsing
   rice wine
1 teaspoon sugar
2 teaspoons sesame oil
1 teaspoon salt

1 Clean the chicken and place in a large saucepan with enough water to cover it. Add the spring onions, ginger and peppercorns; bring to the boil and skim. Add the salt, then cover with a tight-fitting lid and simmer over a low heat for 20–25 minutes.

2 Remove from the heat and leave the chicken to cook gently in the hot liquid, without lifting the lid, for 3–4 hours, or until the liquid is quite cool.

3 To serve, remove the chicken and drain well, reserving the cooking liquid. Either pull the meat off the bone and cut into small pieces, or chop through the bone into bite-sized pieces, then reassemble on a serving dish.

4 Combine the sauce ingredients with about 3 tablespoons of the cooking liquid and bring to the boil. Pour evenly all over the chicken and serve cold.

CHAR SIU

These strips of shining red meat are most often seen hanging in the windows of Chinese restaurants. The traditional way of cooking Char Siu is to skewer the strips of meat at one end, hook them onto the top rack of a specially constructed oven and roast them in suspension. Here is an alternative method for a domestic oven.

900g fillet of pork
225g Hoi Sin (Chinese barbecue)
  sauce
1½ tablespoons Shao Hsing rice
  wine or brandy
1 teaspoon sesame oil
1½ tablespoons honey, thinned
  down with a little water

1 Cut the pork into strips about 18–20cm long.

2 Marinate in the Hoi Sin sauce, wine and sesame oil in a shallow dish, covered, for at least 8–12 hours.

3 Preheat the oven to 220°C/425°F/gas 7. Place a baking tin filled with about 575ml boiling water at the bottom of the oven. Take the pork strips out of the marinade and drain (reserving the marinade). Place the meat flat on a wire rack and roast on the top shelf of the oven for 15–20 minutes, allowing the juices to drip into the pan of water. Baste with the marinade, reduce the oven temperature to 180°C/350°F/gas 4 and continue roasting for a further 20–25 minutes.

4 Remove the meat from the oven and brush with the honey. Return the meat to the oven and cook for a further 4–5 minutes to crisp the outside a little and give it a rich colour.

5 When the meat is quite cool, slice it across the grain just before serving; this preserves the flavour and moist texture. Bring the marinade to a boil with the drippings and water in the baking pan; simmer gently for a few minutes and strain into a jug to serve with the meat.

SOY-BRAISED DUCK

1 duck, weighing 2kg
2 teaspoons salt
3–4 star anise
2 cinnamon sticks
1 teaspoon Sichuan peppercorns
2–3 spring onions, each tied into
 a knot
3–4 slices fresh ginger root,
 crushed
115g rock candy or crystal sugar
3 tablespoons Shao Hsing rice
 wine or brandy
75ml light soy sauce
3 tablespoons dark soy sauce
1.1 litres water

1 Clean the duck well, then blanch in boiling water. Remove and rinse in cold water, and rub the cavity with the salt.

2 Put all the remaining ingredients in a large saucepan, add the water and bring to the boil. Add the duck, breast-side down, bring back to the boil, then reduce the heat and simmer, covered, for 20 minutes. Turn the bird over and cook, still covered, for a further 20 minutes.

3 Turn off the heat and let the bird cool in the liquid, without lifting the lid, for at least 3–4 hours.

4 To serve, remove the duck and drain. Chop into small bite-sized pieces and use a little of the strained liquid as a sauce.

BAKED WHOLE FISH

Salmon or turbot steaks can also be used for this recipe.

1 scaled and gutted carp, sea
   bass, trout or grey mullet,
   weighing about 700g
½ teaspoon salt
1 teaspoon sesame oil
2–3 spring onions, finely
   shredded
2–3 slices fresh ginger root,
   finely shredded
1 tablespoon crushed black
   beans
1 tablespoon light soy sauce
1 tablespoon Shao Hsing
   rice wine
coriander leaves to garnish

1 Clean and dry the fish well. Score both sides as far as the bone with diagonal cuts at 1cm intervals and rub the inside with the salt (this process is unnecessary if you're cooking fish steaks instead of a whole fish).

2 Preheat the oven to 200°C/400°F/ gas 6. Grease a double-folded large sheet of tinfoil with the sesame oil and place the fish on top of a few strips of spring onions and ginger. Mix the crushed black beans with the soy sauce and wine, spread out evenly all over the fish and then add the rest of the spring onions and ginger. Fold and double-fold the edges of the tinfoil to form a loose parcel, pinching together the edges so that liquids will not run out.

3 Cook the fish in the preheated oven for 25–30 minutes.

4 To serve, unwrap the parcel carefully when cool and garnish with coriander leaves.

FRIED RICE

350g long-grain rice
450ml cold water
2 teaspoons salt
115g cooked and peeled prawns
115g cooked ham
3–4 eggs
2–3 spring onions,
    finely chopped
3 tablespoons oil
115g green peas

1 Place the rice in a saucepan with the water and a pinch of salt, bring to the boil and stir once to prevent it sticking to the bottom of the pan. Reduce the heat to very low, cover with a tight-fitting lid and cook for 15 minutes. Fluff the rice up with a fork or spoon then leave to cool until hard.

2 Pat the prawns dry and cut the ham into small pea-sized cubes. Beat the eggs with a pinch of salt and a few bits of the finely chopped spring onions.

3 Heat the oil in a wok and lightly scramble the eggs. Add the prawns, ham and peas and stir-fry for about 1 minute; then add the rice with the remaining salt and spring onions. Blend well, stirring to separate each grain. Serve hot or cold.

SPONGE CAKE

Traditionally, this cake is made with nine layers, each layer a different colour. Here is a simplified version of a single, one-colour layer.

4 eggs
115g caster sugar
100ml milk
225g self-raising flour
½ teaspoon bicarbonate of soda
pinch of salt
30g lard
3 tablespoons vegetable oil

1 Beat the eggs in a bowl. Add the sugar and continue beating until the mixture is thick and pale in colour. Stir in the milk. Sift together the flour, soda and salt and fold into the egg mixture.

2 Melt the lard and allow to cool, then mix with the oil. Gently stir into the egg mixture. Pour into a greased 20cm round cake tin and steam for 20 minutes. Remove the cake from the tin while still hot and cool on a rack.

3 Cut the cake into 6–8 wedges and serve.

DRAGON BOAT FESTIVAL

On the fifth day of the fifth moon, dragon boat races are held all over China, when long paddle-boats, garishly decorated as dragons, compete against each other to commemorate the anniversary of Chu Yuan's death.

An honest, upright poet-statesman full of integrity, Chu Yuan drowned himself in the river Miluo Jiang in Hunan province in 295 BC in protest against the corruption of the government. The people were so upset that they took to their boats to search for his body. They threw rice and eggs into the water in an attempt to draw away the fishes, hoping the fish would prefer to nibble them rather than Chu Yuan's mortal remains. As a reminder people still eat Zong Zi, a form of dumpling made of glutinous rice wrapped in bamboo leaves, and salted eggs.

left Dragon Boat racing, Christian Keenan/Getty Images

ZONG ZI

GLUTINOUS RICE WRAPPED IN BAMBOO LEAVES

From the wide range of different fillings for Zong Zi, here are two, one sweet and one savoury. For instructions on how to wrap Zong Zi in bamboo leaves see page 56.

SWEET FILLING FOR 12 ZONG ZI
900g glutinous rice
1 tablespoon oil
450g sweet black bean paste

1 For the sweet filling, soak the rice for 2 hours, drain and change the water. Soak for a further 30 minutes, then drain well. Mix in the oil.

2 Roll the black bean paste into a sausage about 2.5cm in diameter. Cut into 12 sections, and flatten each slightly.

SAVOURY FILLING FOR 12 ZONG ZI
450g glutinous rice
75ml oil
1 teaspoon salt
6–8 Chinese dried mushrooms
225g dried chestnuts
1½ tablespoons dried shrimps
285–350g Char Siu pork, or ham
2–3 salted duck egg yolks, or
  hard-boiled egg yolks
½ teaspoon sugar
1 tablespoon Shao Hsing
  rice wine
1 tablespoon light soy sauce
1½ tablespoons finely chopped
  spring onions

1 For the savoury filling, soak the rice for 2 hours, drain and change the water. Soak for a further 30 minutes, then drain well. Mix with about one third of the oil and half the salt.

2 Soak the dried mushrooms in warm water for 20–25 minutes, the dried chestnuts for 25–30 minutes and the dried shrimps for 20 minutes. Squeeze the mushrooms dry, discard the stalks and then cut into small cubes the same size as the shrimps. Peel the chestnuts and dice with the pork or ham. Rinse and drain the shrimps. Chop the egg yolks and set aside.

3 Heat the remaining oil in a wok, stir-fry all the ingredients except the egg yolks, add the seasonings and spring onions and blend well. Set aside.

TO WRAP ZONG ZI
IN BAMBOO LEAVES

48 dried bamboo leaves
24 strings, each about
    15m long

1 Soak the bamboo leaves in warm water for 2–3 hours, rinse in fresh water then drain and wipe dry.

2 Place two leaves side by side, slightly overlapping; fold the two bottoms over together to form a triangular pouch. Add a portion of the rice and place a piece of the bean paste on the rice if making sweet Zong Zi; or place some of the savoury filling with a few bits of the chopped egg yolks if making savoury Zong Zi. Cover the filling with more rice and fold the leaves over the top and round the pouch to produce a plump, triangular-shaped bundle. Tie securely with string. Leave a little leeway when wrapping up the bundle as the rice will expand during cooking.

3 To cook, bring a large saucepan or wok of water to a rolling boil, drop in the Zong Zi and simmer gently for 2–3 hours. Cook the sweet and savoury Zong Zi in separate pans.

4 To serve, open the Zong Zi packages at the table and serve hot. Extra sugar may be required for the sweet ones, and salt and pepper for the savoury ones. Any leftovers can be reheated, but they must be unwrapped; they usually taste even better than the first time.

FIVE-SPICE TEA EGGS

The egg represents fertility and its round smooth shape symbolises good luck and happiness. It also features prominently in many of the Chinese festivals as an offering to the Gods. According to legend, when the world began the universe was egg-shaped, the yolk representing the earth and the white the heavens. Then *Pan-ku*, primal man, separated them and the bright and clear element – *yang* – became heaven and the dark and murky *yin* formed the earth.

12 eggs
1 teaspoon salt
3 tablespoons light or dark
  soy sauce
2–3 star anise, or 1 teaspoon
  five-spice powder
3 tablespoons black China
  tea leaves

1 Hard-boil the eggs for 6–8 minutes. Drain and tap the shells gently with a spoon or roll the eggs on a hard surface until they are cracked finely all over.

2 Put the eggs back in the saucepan, cover with fresh water, add the salt, soy sauce, spice and tea leaves. Bring to the boil and simmer for about 45–50 minutes. Allow the eggs to cool in the liquid.

3 To serve, shell the eggs to reveal a beautiful marbled pattern.

THE LOTUS FESTIVAL

The Lotus Festival is celebrated on the twenty-fourth day of the sixth moon. It also coincides with the coming of the summer rains when the parched earth is revitalized and the ripening crops receive much-needed moisture.

The red lotus (*Nelumbium speciosum*) grows in lakes, ponds and marshes and is particularly beautiful after a shower as drops of water collect at the base of its jade-green leaves and shine like diamonds in the sun. No wonder the crowds row in little boats to admire the sumptuous pink flowers.

Flowers have always been used by artists throughout China to represent the four seasons: the summer flower is the lotus blossom, for autumn the chrysanthemum, for winter plum blossom, and for spring the peony.

The lotus blossom is also closely associated with Buddha. The essence of the Buddhist doctrine is universal redemption and the lotus has come to symbolise man raising himself above the material world to realise his divine nature – for although the lotus grows in mud, it emerges in gorgeous splendour in full bloom.
Its roots, fruits and leaves are all edible; sliced fresh roots are added to stir-fried vegetables, dried leaves are mainly used for wrapping, the seeds, which have medicinal value, make one of the best sweetmeats, and the kernels or lotus-nuts are boiled in soup, roasted or eaten raw.

left Elena Segatini/Iconica/Getty Images

STEAMED PORK WITH GROUND RICE

Traditionally the pork is steamed on a bed of lotus leaves in a bamboo steamer. But here is an alternative method.

675g belly pork, boned but
  with skin on
½ teaspoon salt
1½ tablespoons light soy sauce
1 teaspoon sugar
1 tablespoon Shao Hsing
  rice wine
115g ground rice
1–2 star anise

1 Cut the pork into cubes and marinate in the salt, soy sauce, sugar and wine for 20–25 minutes.

2 Brown the rice and star anise in a wok or frying pan over medium heat until golden, remove and crush with a rolling pin until fine. Coat each piece of pork with the ground rice, pressing it in well.

3 Arrange the pork in one layer, skin-side down, in a bowl or dish. Steam vigorously for at least 4–5 hours, or until the meat is very tender.

4 To serve, turn the meat onto a dish so that the skin side faces up. Serve hot with additional seasonings such as soy sauce and chilli sauce.

DOUBLE SEVENTH FESTIVAL

On the seventh day of the seventh moon, unmarried girls celebrate the Double Seventh Festival by making offerings to the Weaver Maid. Ancient folklore has it that once upon a time Cowherd the orphan was banished into the wilderness by his wicked sister-in-law. All he was allowed to take with him was an old buffalo that he had once rescued from starvation. The buffalo turned into a Fairy Godmother and produced a magic bean that grew up into the skies. Cowherd climbed the stalk and when he reached the heavens discovered the King and Queen's seven daughters bathing in the celestial pool.

On the instructions of the Fairy Godmother he ran off with the clothes of Weaver Maid, daughter number seven, and the prettiest of all. She was forced to descend to earth to retrieve her modesty, and once there found herself in such a compromising position that she had no choice but to marry Cowherd.

During three very happy years she bore Cowherd twins and taught the earth maidens how to weave silk and to embroider, but her parents decided that it was high time she returned to the fold before she was too corrupted by earthly pleasure and so her mother came down to earth and dragged her away. Cowherd and the twins ran after her and almost caught up with her, but the Queen drew a line across the heaven with a stroke of her silver pin and formed the Celestial River or Milky Way to separate the lovers for ever. The King, moved by the sound of their weeping, took pity on them and consented to allow them to be reunited once a year on the Double Seventh. On this night the magpies flock together to form a bridge with their wings over the Milky Way and young girls offer gifts of watermelon, luscious fruit and sweetmeats and, in return, beg the Weaver Maid for help and guidance in their needlework.

left Woman with cattle, Yunnan Province, The Image Bank/Getty Images

FRUIT SALAD IN WATERMELON

Seven different fruits are used for this Double Seventh Festival recipe.

225g rock candy or crystal sugar
  (optional)
575ml water (optional)
1 small watermelon
6 fruits from the following:
  pineapple, pears, grapes,
  lychees, tangerines, peaches,
  banana, cherries, papaya,
  mango, kiwi fruit

1 If no tinned fruit with syrup is used, dissolve the rock candy in boiling water, then cool.

2 Slice about 5cm off the top of the watermelon and scoop out the flesh, discarding the seeds; cut the flesh into small chunks. Prepare the other fresh fruits by cutting them into small chunks.

3 Fill the watermelon shell with fruits and syrup. Chill and serve cold.

FESTIVAL OF THE HUNGRY GHOSTS

The Festival of the Hungry Ghosts dates from the first century AD, when Buddhism was first introduced to China. It is held on the fifteenth day of the seventh moon in honour of the unhappy dead or 'orphaned spirits' – those who have died far from home, or have drowned, or have neither a marked grave nor descendants to perpetuate their memory.

Vegetarian food, in the Buddhist tradition, is offered to the hungry ghosts to assuage their pangs and gain their gratitude, for unless they are pacified by food they seek living substitutes. It is also customary to burn paper clothing and money to appease the spirits and, in some parts of China, lanterns are lit to help wandering ghosts find their way.

right Buddha statue, Michele Westmorland/The Image Bank/Getty Images

TEN-VARIETY VEGETABLES

The Chinese never mix ingredients indiscriminately, but select carefully to achieve a harmonious balance of colour, aroma, flavour and texture.

4–6 Chinese dried mushrooms, soaked for 30–40 minutes in warm water
100g bean curd (tofu)
55g mange tout or French beans
55g water chestnuts
125g each of Chinese leaves, cauliflower, courgettes, carrots, white mushrooms, fresh beansprouts
60ml oil
1 teaspoon sesame oil
1 teaspoon salt
1 teaspoon sugar
1½ tablespoons light soy sauce

1 Squeeze the mushrooms dry (reserving the water) and discard the stalks. Half or quarter them according to their size.

2 Cut the bean curd into about 12 small pieces, then harden the pieces in a pot of lightly salted boiling water for 2–3 minutes. Remove and drain.

3 Top and tail the mange tout or French beans; leave whole if small, snap in half if large. Cut the other vegetables into a roughly uniform size, except the beansprouts, which need only be washed and rinsed.

4 Heat about half the oil in a flameproof casserole or saucepan and lightly brown the bean curd pieces on both sides. Remove with a slotted spoon and set aside.

5 Heat the remaining oil and sesame oil and stir-fry the rest of the vegetables for about 2 minutes. Add the bean curd with the salt, sugar, soy sauce and a little of the mushroom-soaking water; stir to blend well, cover, reduce the heat and simmer for 4–5 minutes.

THE MID-AUTUMN FESTIVAL

Around the time of the autumnal equinox, on the fifteenth day of the eighth moon, there is the Mid-autumn or Moon Festival.

Yue Lao, the 'Old Man in the Moon' is also the universal match-maker. This is the night when he and his little white rabbit helper are busily engaged binding couples together with invisible red silk thread. According to an old saying the mid-autumn moon always shines extra brightly as 'the sky is high and the weather crisp and fine' and everyone celebrates with gifts of fruit, sweets and, of course, moon cakes.

left Masao Ota/Amana Images/Getty Images

MOON CAKES

During the Mongol rule in China in 1271–1368 guards were billeted in every household to watch for signs of uprising. The Chinese, however, would not be suppressed. By sending messages hidden inside moon cakes they were able to plot and scheme to overthrow the invaders.

Moon Cakes are golden brown pastry pies enclosing any number of fillings to suit all pockets and tastes and stamped on top with the emblem of the deity.

MOON CAKES HOME-STYLE

PASTRY A
285g flour
170g lard, softened
about 150ml water
10ml sugar
pinch of salt

PASTRY B
170g flour
170g lard, softened

FILLING
450g sweet red bean paste

1 Sift the flour for pastry A into a mixing bowl and add the lard and water. Slowly work in and add the sugar and salt. Knead until smooth.

2 Sift the flour for pastry B into another bowl. Add the lard. Work in and knead until smooth. On a lightly dusted surface, roll the two doughs into two 'sausages', then divide each into 24 portions.

3 Roll each portion into a round ball and flatten with a rolling pin, making the pastry A circles larger than those of B. Place the pastry B circles on top of the A circles. Fold four edges of the A over the B pastry to form a square, and gently roll out into a rectangular shape. Fold the two ends into the centre to form a square again, then lightly roll out into a circular shape, fairly thin.

4 When all the pastry cases are made, divide the red bean paste into 24 portions and roll each into a small ball, then flatten slightly. Place one in the centre of each circle of pastry and pull the edges together to enclose the paste. Brush with a little water or beaten egg if the edges do not stick well.

5 Preheat the oven to 200°C/400°F/gas 6. Place the cakes on a greased and floured baking tray. Bake in the oven for about 20 minutes. Remove and serve cold.

DOUBLE NINTH FESTIVAL

The ninth day of the ninth moon is celebrated as the Double Ninth Festival throughout China. It is also known as the Festival of Mounting the Heights (Deng Kao), and it is considered lucky to climb to a high place to take in the clear, fresh air. Kite-flying is a popular spectacle on the hilltops on this day; and since almost all ancestral tombs are on the high grounds the people take this opportunity to pay a visit and clear the summer growth from the graves. Sacrifices are offered, after which worshippers picnic in the open, as they did for the Qing Ming Festival.

left Kites, Charles Bowman/Robert Harding World Imagery/Getty Images

DRUNKEN CHICKEN

Be sure to use a young chicken for this;
never use a frozen chicken.

1 young chicken,
  weighing 1.35kg
2 litres water
1 tablespoon salt
2–3 spring onions, cut into
  short lengths
3–4 slices fresh ginger root,
  peeled
2 teaspoons Sichuan peppercorns
3–4 star anise
3 tablespoons Shao Hsing
  rice wine
100ml Gao Liang (sorghum)
  spirit, brandy or whisky

1 Clean the chicken well, then blanch in a pot of boiling water for 2–3 minutes. Remove and rinse in cold water.

2 Bring the water to the boil with the salt, spring onions, ginger, Sichuan peppercorns, star anise and rice wine. Place the chicken in the liquid, reduce heat and simmer, covered, for 35–40 minutes; leave to cool.

3 Joint the chicken into four quarters. Strain the liquid, mix with the spirit and pour over the chicken pieces; leave to marinate, covered, for 5–6 hours.

4 To serve, chop the chicken into bite-sized pieces, pour over a little of the marinade and serve cold.

COLD TOSSED NOODLES

Spices in Chinese food almost certainly have religious connections, cleansing the body and purifying the soul.

55g dried shrimps
3 tablespoons Shao Hsing
   rice wine
350g egg noodles
1 tablespoon oil
170g fresh beansprouts
3–4 slices fresh ginger root,
   thinly shredded
3 tablespoons light soy sauce
1½ tablespoons vinegar
2 teaspoons sugar
1 teaspoon red chilli oil
   (optional)
finely shredded spring onions
   to garnish
1 teaspoon sesame oil, to garnish

1 Soak the dried shrimps in hot water for 5 minutes, rinse and drain, then coarsely chop and marinate in the rice wine for 15 minutes.

2 Cook the noodles in a pan of boiling water following the instructions on the packet. Rinse in cold water and drain, then add the oil and mix well.

3 Blanch the beansprouts, then rinse in cold water. Drain and set aside.

4 Gently heat the shredded ginger, soy sauce, vinegar, sugar and chilli oil with a little water to make a sauce.

5 To serve, spread the noodles on a large serving dish. Sprinkle over the beansprouts, the chopped shrimps and wine, shredded spring onions and sesame oil. Finally, pour over the sauce, toss and serve.

FIVE-SPICED SPARE RIBS

1kg pork, lamb or veal spare ribs

MARINADE
1 tablespoon sugar
1½ tablespoons light soy sauce
2 garlic cloves, crushed
50ml Shao Hsing rice wine
   or brandy
2 teaspoons five-spice powder
75ml Hoi Sin (Chinese
   barbecue) sauce

1 Trim off any excess fat from the ribs and cut into individual pieces. Combine the marinade ingredients and pour over the ribs in a baking dish; marinate for 2–3 hours, turning occasionally.

2 Preheat the oven to 230°C/450°F/gas 8. Roast the ribs for 15 minutes, then add a little water (about 100ml) and reduce the heat to 200°C/400°F/gas 6; cook for another 30–35 minutes, turning once or twice. Serve hot or cold.

CRAB WITH SPRING ONIONS AND GINGER

2 medium-sized crabs,
   each weighing
   about 400g
60ml oil
3–4 spring onions,
   cut into long strips
4–5 slices fresh ginger root,
   finely chopped
½ teaspoon salt
1 tablespoon sugar
1½ tablespoons Shao Hsing
   rice wine
1½ tablespoons light
   soy sauce
1 tablespoon vinegar
2 teaspoons cornflour
   blended with an equal
   amount of cold water
spring onions cut diagonally
   to garnish

1 Break off the legs and crack the claws of the crabs. Wash off any mud and green matter both outside and inside the shell, and discard the feathery gills and the sac. Break the body into two or three pieces.

2 Heat the oil in a wok and fry the crab pieces until golden. Remove and drain.

3 Add the spring onions and ginger to what is left of the oil in the wok; add the salt, sugar, wine, soy sauce, vinegar and a little stock or water. Bring to the boil, return the crab pieces to be coated by the sauce. Braise for 2–3 minutes, then thicken the sauce with the cornflour-and-water mixture; blend well. Serve hot or cold garnished with spring onions.

BIRTHDAY OF
THE CITY GODS

The twenty-fifth day of the ninth moon is the
anniversary of the City Gods, whose duties are to care
for the souls of their dead parishioners and ward off
epidemics and disasters. Every walled town in China
would have at least one temple built specially for their
patron saints, and during this important religious
festival crowds used to gather in the temple
compounds, and stalls and stands selling all kinds of
commodity would be set up. The highlight would be a
parade through the town, with colourful floats,
tableaux, firecrackers and music.

Though no particular dish would have been eaten
during this period, the following recipe is one of the
best items sold by the street vendors.

right A dragon lantern at the festival, Kevin R Morris/Bohemian
Nomad Picturemakers/Corbis

CRISPY VEGETARIAN SPRING ROLLS

1 packet of 20 frozen spring
  roll skins
225g fresh beansprouts
115g each of tender leeks or
  spring onions, carrots, bamboo
  shoots, white mushrooms
1 teaspoon salt
1 teaspoon sugar
1 tablespoon light soy sauce
1 tablespoon Shao sing rice
  wine (optional)
1 tablespoon plain flour mixed
  with equal amount of water
about 575ml oil for deep-frying

1 Take the spring roll skins out of the packet and defrost thoroughly.

2 Wash and rinse the beansprouts in cold water, discard the husks and drain. Shred all the vegetables to roughly the same size as the beansprouts.

3 Heat about 3 tablespoons oil in a wok or frying-pan and stir-fry the vegetables for about 1 minute, then add the salt, sugar, soy sauce and wine (if using), and continue cooking for a further 1–1 1/2 minutes, stirring continuously. Remove and leave to cool.

4 To make the spring rolls: cut each spring roll skin in half diagonally, and, with the triangle pointing away from you, place one teaspoon of the vegetables about a third of the way down the skin, lift the lower flap over the filling and roll once, then fold over both ends and roll once more. Brush the upper edge with a little flour-and-water paste, and roll into a neat package. Repeat until all the filling is used up. Lightly dust a tray with flour and place the spring rolls in rows with the flap-side down. (They can be kept in the refrigerator for a day or two, or they can be frozen for up to six months.)

5 To cook, heat the remaining oil until smoking, then reduce the heat or even turn it off for a while. Deep-fry the spring rolls 6–8 at a time for 3–4 minutes, or until golden and crispy; remove and drain. Increase the heat to high again before frying the next batch.

6 Serve hot with a dipping sauce such as soy sauce, vinegar, chilli sauce or salt and pepper.

TOFFEE WATER CHESTNUTS

Fresh water chestnuts (as opposed to tinned ones) are available during the late autumn and winter months in the Chinatown districts of both the United States and Britain.

450g water chestnuts
10–12 bamboo skewers (satay
   sticks), soaked in water for
   25–30 minutes
1 tablespoon oil
115g caster sugar
3 tablespoons fruit syrup
about 1 tablespoon hot water

1 Wash and scrape the water chestnuts but do not peel them. Boil in a pan of water for 4–5 minutes, then remove and drain. (If using tinned water chestnuts, they are already peeled and cooked, so just rinse and drain.) Thread about 6–8 water chestnuts onto each bamboo stick.

2 Heat the oil in a frying pan, add the sugar, syrup and water. Bring to the boil, then reduce the heat and stir until the sugar is caramelised. Add the skewers and turn until the water chestnuts are covered all over with the toffee. Serve hot or cold.

FESTIVAL OF THE WINTER SOLSTICE

The chief festival during the eleventh moon is the Winter Solstice or Dong Zhi. It marks the turning point of the year – the passing of the shortest day – and the dying year also evokes memories of the dead. The Chinese believe that ghosts are much busier during the longest night so great preparations are made for their visit.

A lavish feast is laid out before the ancestral altar, empty chairs for the spirits are set at the head of the table and they are invited to join in the feast. After a few moments of respectful silence the living members of the household all sit down and tuck in.

right Devotees perform a ritual,
Ted Aljibe/AFP/Getty Images

EIGHT-TREASURE RICE PUDDING

Eight-treasure Rice Pudding corresponds to the English Christmas pudding as a national dish and it is traditionally made by a new bride who has married into the family during the year. The Chinese are delightfully vague about the pudding's eight treasures, which might include different kinds of sugar and whole grains (never meal or flour), beans, dates, nuts and fruits.

300ml water
225g glutinous rice
1½ tablespoons sugar
115g lard
15 dried red dates (jujubes), stoned
30 raisins
20 split almonds, chopped
10 candied cherries
10 pieces angelica, chopped
225g red bean paste

SYRUP
50g sugar
150ml water
2 teaspoons cornflour blended with equal amount of water

1 Bring the water and rice to the boil, reduce the heat, cover and cook for 10–15 minutes, or until the water is absorbed. Add the sugar and about half the lard. Mix well.

2 Brush a 900ml capacity mould or pudding basin with the remaining lard. Cover the bottom and sides with a thin layer of the rice mixture. Gently press a layer of the fruit and nuts, attractively arranged in neat rows, into the rice so they will show when the pudding is turned out.

3 Cover the fruit and nuts with another layer of rice, much thicker this time. Fill the centre with the red bean paste and cover with the remaining rice. Press gently to flatten the top. Cover with greaseproof paper or tinfoil.

4 Steam the pudding for 1 hour. A few minutes before serving, make the syrup: dissolve the sugar in the water in a small saucepan, bring to the boil and stir in the cornflour and water mixture; simmer gently, stirring, until thickened.

5 To serve, invert the pudding onto a warmed plate. Pour over the syrup and serve immediately.

THE SACRIFICIAL MOON

The Sacrificial or twelfth moon is known as *la yue*. This is the time of year for 'sweeping the house', re-lacquering the front gates in vermillion red (the colour for good luck and rejoicing) and whitewashing the outer walls and re-papering the windows.

The eighth day is celebrated as a preliminary New Year Festival with a thick porridge called La ba zhou for breakfast. Made from cereals – millet, wheat, sorghum, corn and several kinds of rice - and lentils, nuts and dried fruit, it is first offered to the Ancestral Tablets before being eaten by the family. Sometimes a bowl is sent as a gift to friends or family, in which case it has to arrive before the first stroke of noon.

This is also when the laying in of provisions for the New Year starts. Cured meat such as bacon, sausages or duck are made in great quantities and hung up outside to dry in the winter sun.

PICKLED VEGETABLES

Green vegetables are in short supply at this time of the year, so
any surplus is pickled or preserved for the long winter months.

2.25 litres water, boiled and
  cooled
115g salt
55g chilli peppers
30g Sichuan peppercorns
115g fresh ginger root, peeled
  and sliced
115g sugar
150ml Chinese distilled
  spirit, or brandy, rum,
  whisky
225–285g each of any five of the
  following: radish or turnip,
  carrot, Chinese leaves, green
  and/or white cabbage,
  cauliflower, celery, onion, leek,
  spring onion (white parts
  only), garlic cloves

1 Put the water into a large, clean earthenware or glass
jar. Add the salt, chillies, peppercorns, ginger, sugar and
spirit.

2 Wash and trim the vegetables, peel if necessary and
dry well. Put them into the jar and seal it, making sure it
is airtight. Place the jar in a cool place and leave the
vegetables to pickle for at least five to six days before
serving.

2 Use a pair of clean chopsticks or tongs to pick the
vegetables out of the jar. Do not allow any grease to
enter the jar. You can replenish the vegetables, adding a
little more salt each time. If a white scum appears on the
surface of the brine, add a little more sugar and spirit.
The longer the pickling lasts, the better the taste.

PORK SAUSAGES

These strings of rosy sausages seen hanging in the windows of
Chinese restaurants are akin to the continental salami or saucisson.

675g lean pork
225g pork fat
1 tablespoon salt
1½ tablespoons sugar
1 teaspoon five-spice powder
1½ tablespoons light
    or dark soy sauce
150ml Shao Hsing rice wine
    or brandy
about 3m sausage (chipolata
    size) casing
22 strings, each about 10cm long

1 Coarsely chop the pork and fat and marinate in the salt,
sugar, spice, soy sauce and wine for at least 8 hours or
overnight.

2 Carefully attach the casing to the end of a funnel, and
tie the other end of the casing with string. Push the meat
mixture into the casing through the funnel and squeeze to
distribute the meat evenly throughout. The sausage should
be loosely packed. Once all the meat has been stuffed
into the casing, tie off the funnel end. Tie the casing at
15cm intervals and prick the sausage all over with a
fine pin.

3 Hang the sausage in an airy place to dry for at least
3–4 days, or the process can be hastened by using a fan
heater for 24–36 hours.

4 When completely dry, store the sausages in the
refrigerator; they will keep for weeks if wrapped airtight,
and up to six months in the freezer.

5 To serve, cut into thin diagonal slices and fry in a little oil
until the fat bits turn translucent; or, better still, steam on top
of rice for 10–15 minutes.